W9-BZP-776

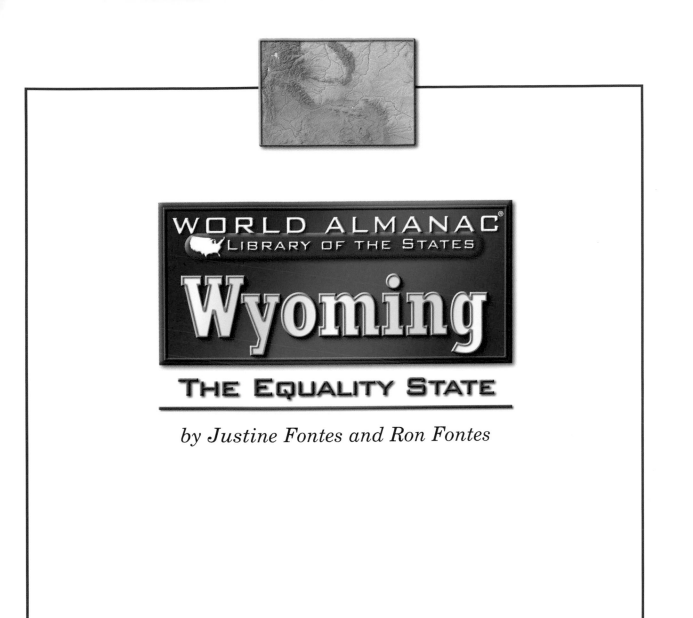

WORLD ALMANAC®
LIBRARY OF THE STATES

Wyoming

THE EQUALITY STATE

by Justine Fontes and Ron Fontes

WORLD ALMANAC® LIBRARY

Please visit our web site at: www.worldalmanaclibrary.com
For a free color catalog describing World Almanac® Library's list of high-quality books
and multimedia programs, call 1-800-848-2928 (USA) or 1-800-387-3178 (Canada).
World Almanac® Library's fax: (414) 332-3567.

Library of Congress Cataloging-in-Publication Data

Korman, Justine.
    Wyoming, the Equality State / by Justine and Ron Fontes.
       p. cm. — (World Almanac Library of the states)
    Includes bibliographical references and index.
    Summary: Describes the history, people, geography, economy, government,
state events and attractions, and social life and customs of Wyoming.
    ISBN 0-8368-5164-1 (lib. bdg.)
    ISBN 0-8368-5335-0 (softcover)
    1. Wyoming—Juvenile literature. [1. Wyoming.] I. Fontes, Ron. II. Title.
III. Series.
F761.3.K67   2003
978.7—dc21   2002191003

First published in 2003 by
World Almanac® Library
330 West Olive Street, Suite 100
Milwaukee, WI 53212 USA

Copyright © 2003 by World Almanac® Library.

A Creative Media Applications Production
Design: Alan Barnett, Inc.
Copyeditor: Laurie Lieb
Fact Checker: Joan Verniero
Photo Researcher: Linette Mathewson
World Almanac® Library project editor: Tim Paulson
World Almanac® Library editors: Mary Dykstra, Gustav Gedatus, Jacqueline Laks Gorman,
  Lyman Lyons
World Almanac® Library art direction: Tammy Gruenewald
World Almanac® Library graphic designers: Scott M. Krall, Melissa Valuch

Photo credits: p. 4 © David R. Frazier/Danita Delimont, Agent; p. 6 (top right) © Artoday; p. 6
(bottom left) © Artoday; p. 6 (bottom right) © Jonathan Blair/CORBIS; p. 7 (top) © Bruce
Coleman; p. 7 (bottom) © AP/Wide World Photographs; p. 09 © John Elk III; p. 10 © Northwind
Archives; p. 11 © Photri, Inc.; p. 12 © North Wind Archives; p. 13 © AP/Wide World
Photographs; p. 14 © Jack Olson; p. 15 © Photri, Inc.; p. 17 © AP/Wide World Photographs;
p. 18 © Dave G. Houser/CORBIS; p. 19 © Bruce Coleman; p. 20 (left) © Steve Kaufman/CORBIS ;
p. 20 (center) © AP/Wide World Photographs; p. 20 (right) © Bruce Coleman; p. 21 (left) © Craig
Lovell; p. 21 (center) © Jack Olson; p. 21 (right) © Buddy Mays; p. 23 © Buddy Mays; p. 26
© Buddy Mays; p. 27 © Jonathan Blair/CORBIS ; p. 29 © David R. Frazier/Danita Delimont,
Agent; p. 31 (top) © AP/Wide World Photographs; p. 31 (bottom) © AP/Wide World Photographs;
p. 32 © Jon Elk III; p. 33 © Walter Bibikow/Danita Delimont, Agent; p. 34 © Jon Elk III; p. 35
© Jon Elk III; p. 36 © Hulton Archive/Getty Images; p. 37 (top) © Photri, Inc.; p. 37 (bottom)
© AP Photo/Susan Sterner; p. 38 © Hulton Archives/Getty Images; p. 39 (left) © North Wind
Archives; p. 39 (right) © Photri, Inc.; p. 40 © Photri, Inc.; p. 41 © Photri, Inc.; p. 4243 © Photri,
Inc.; p. 44 (top) © John Elk III; p. 44 (bottom) © AP/Wide World Photographs; p. 45 (top) © Paul
A. Souders/CORBIS ; p. 45 (bottom) © AP/Wide World Photographs.

Printed in the United States of America

1 2 3 4 5 6 7 8 9 07 06 05 04 03

Wyoming

Past and Future

The cowboy way of life lasted only about twenty years, from the 1870s through the 1880s, but like the scrappy, low grass that struggles to survive on Wyoming's sun-baked plains, the cowboy tradition stays alive. More than just the hat and boots, cowboy life is an attitude: a willingness to accept hard work and tough living conditions; an appreciation of nature, even at its cruelest; an easy laugh; and a tendency to swagger.

Wyoming is indeed, as the old song goes, a

"Home on the range,
   Where the deer and the antelope play,
Where seldom is heard a discouraging word
   And the skies are not cloudy all day."

Many Wyomingites still live "on the range," raising cattle. Others earn their living from the land by mining or farming. Most have more modern jobs in the service sector. But even if they have traded their horses for pickup trucks or SUVs, Wyomingites still retain the cowboy hat — and the attitude.

Despite some development over the years, Wyoming remains a refuge for deer, antelope, and all kinds of wildlife, including grizzly bears, bison, and bighorn sheep. The state is blessed with more than its share of natural wonders: a multitude of majestic mountains, dramatic canyons, sparkling waterfalls, world-famous fossil beds, and the gushing geysers of Yellowstone, the nation's first and arguably its finest national park. Wyoming's colorful history includes not only cowboys, but also a wide variety of Native American tribes, wild outlaws, wily mountain men, and the distinction of being the first state to grant women the right to vote.

No other state has so much — and so little: Wyoming has fewer people than any state in the Union. But that's just fine with most Wyomingites, who would rather have room to swing a rope than smell the smoke of another man's fire.

▶ Map of Wyoming showing interstate highway system, as well as major cities and waterways.

▼ Young cowboys and cowgirls still learn to rope and ride on Wyoming's many ranches.

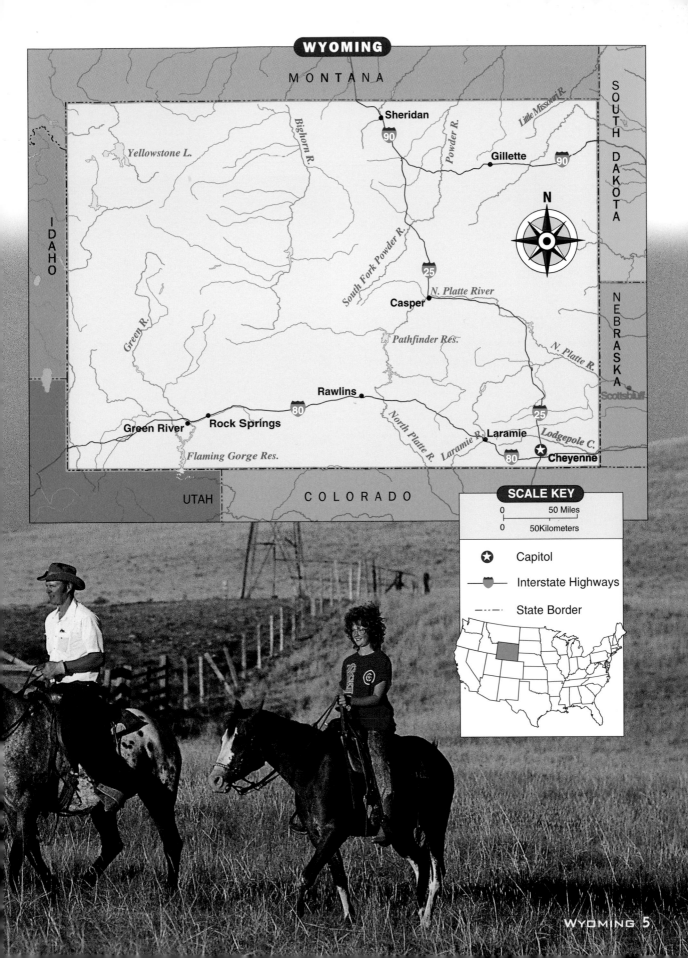

WYOMING

MONTANA

Sheridan

Gillette

Yellowstone L.

Bighorn R.

Powder R.

Little Missouri R.

IDAHO

SOUTH DAKOTA

South Fork Powder R.

N. Platte River

Casper

Green R.

Pathfinder Res.

N. Platte R.

NEBRASKA

Scottsbluff

Rawlins

North Platte R.

Laramie R.

Lodgepole C.

Green River

Rock Springs

Laramie

Cheyenne

Flaming Gorge Res.

UTAH

COLORADO

SCALE KEY

0   50 Miles

0   50 Kilometers

★   Capitol

  Interstate Highways

·–··–·   State Border

Fast Facts

WYOMING (WY), Equality State, Cowboy State

Entered Union

July 10, 1890 (44th state)

Capital	Population
Cheyenne	53,011

Total Population (2000)

493,782 (the least populous state)

— Between 1990 and 2000, the state's population increased 8.9 percent. Wyoming has only about 5 people per square mile (2 per square kilometer)!

Largest Cities	Population
Cheyenne	53,011
Casper	49,644

Land Area

97,100 square miles (251,489 sq km) (9th largest state)

State Name

The name *Wyoming* comes from the Delaware tribe's word for "at the big plains."

State Motto

"Equal Rights"

State Song

"Wyoming" *by Charles E. Winter; music by George E. Knapp, and a second version by Earle R. Clemens.*

State Bird

Western meadowlark

State Fish

Cutthroat trout

State Reptile

Horned toad

State Mammal

American bison

State Dinosaur

Triceratops

State Flower

Indian paintbrush

State Tree

Plains cottonwood

State Gemstone

Jade

State Fossil

Knightia (a fossil fish)

PLACES TO VISIT

Buffalo Bill Historical Center, *Cody*

Four museums display crafts, arts, and artifacts of Western life from guns to tepees. The Whitney Gallery of Western Art displays paintings by George Catlin and Frederic Remington.

Eatons' Ranch, *Outside Sheridan*

When this dude ranch opened in the early 1900s, Eastern tourists loved living the ropin' and ridin' life of a cowboy. They still enjoy it today!

Wyoming Dinosaur Center, *Thermopolis*

See dinosaur remains and the rooms where they are prepared for museum displays. Visit digs where crews uncover new bones — and do some digging yourself!

For other places and events, see p. 44

BIGGEST, BEST, AND MOST

- Yellowstone is the nation's largest and most popular national park. It has more geysers than any other site in the world.

- The Old Faithful Inn at Yellowstone is the world's largest log building.

- One of the largest dinosaur skeletons yet discovered is an apatosaurus in the University of Wyoming's Geological Museum.

STATE FIRSTS

- **1869** Wyoming became the first state to grant women the right to vote.

- **1870** Esther Morris became the first female justice of the peace.

- **1903** The Wapiti Ranger Station became the first ranger station built in the United States. Its name is the Native American word for "elk."

- **1925** Wyoming elected the nation's first female governor, Nellie Davis Tayloe Ross. In 1933, Ross became the nation's first female director of the U.S. Mint.

Yellowstone National Park

Many believe the world's first national park is also the best. Every summer, over three million people marvel at approximately ten thousand "thermal features," including geysers that spurt steaming water, bubbling mud pots, and boiling mineral springs. Yellowstone was founded on a "hot spot" where magma (molten rock) from the planet's core approaches the Earth's crust. The park's most famous geyser, Old Faithful, erupts faithfully about once an hour. The park's wildlife includes some of the country's last grizzly bears, bison, and gray wolves.

WY TM

Wyoming has its own trademark. The Bucking Horse and Rider (BH&R) is a symbol both of the state and its university. The BH&R was first worn by the Wyoming National Guard in France and Germany during World War I (1914–1918). Designed by First Sergeant George N. Ostrom, it was adopted by the U.S. Army as a means of identification on trucks, helmets, and other equipment. Some believe the symbol dates back to the 1900s and a legendary rodeo horse named Steamboat, known as "the horse who couldn't be ridden." In 1936, the BH&R became part of Wyoming's license plate. The symbol is used widely throughout the state, expressing Wyoming's pride in its cowboy past — and present.

The Equality State

> We may stay out of the union a hundred years
> but we will come with our women.
>
> — *The Wyoming legislature in an 1890 telegram to Congress,
> in response to the suggestion that the territory revoke its
> women's right to vote in order to gain statehood*

Seventy-five million years ago, a vast ocean covered Wyoming and much of the land that is now the western United States. Changes in climate caused the ocean to gradually give way to swamp. Forest flourished around the swamp, only to be engulfed when the water rose again. Sediment (dissolved rock particles) in the water seeped into the sunken trees and other debris to form fossils. These impressions left by skeletons, shells, leaves, and blossoms show scientists what kinds of plants and animals lived in Wyoming many thousands of years ago.

The area that is now called Wyoming may have been occupied by people as early as 7000 B.C. Archaeological evidence suggests that these first Wyomingites moved around in search of roots, seeds, and small animals to eat. Then, as the area grew colder and drier, they were forced to leave. Several thousand years later, the ancestors of modern Native Americans arrived, probably following grazing herds. They invented the bow and arrow. Gradually they grew from small families or bands of hunters into large tribes. These traveling hunters lived in buffalo-hide tepees that could easily be taken down and carried when the tribe moved to follow game.

Wyoming's recorded history begins in the early nineteenth century with travelers who encountered tribes known as the Plains Indians. The tribes became partners with early white fur traders, but became increasingly hostile as more outsiders arrived and disrupted their traditional way of life. Except for the Shoshone and Arapaho, all the Plains Indians were driven out of Wyoming by 1878.

Native Americans of Wyoming

Arapaho

Arikara

Bannock

Blackfeet

Cheyenne

Crow

Flathead

Kiowa

Nez Perce

Shoshone

Sioux

Ute

DID YOU KNOW?

Museums all over the world display fossils found in Wyoming. Fossils of triceratops, stegosaurus, apatosaurus, tyrannosaurus, and other dinosaurs are scattered throughout the state.

First Europeans

Some historians believe that fur-trading brothers François and Louis Joseph de La Vérendrye were the first white men to explore Wyoming, in 1743. French-Canadian fur trader François Antoine Larocque became the first authenticated visitor when he traded furs with tribes in the Powder River region in 1805. In 1807, John Colter, leaving the famous Lewis and Clark Expedition to explore the Rocky Mountains, found the region of steaming geysers and towering waterfalls that is now Yellowstone National Park.

Wyoming's fur trade flourished during the 1820s and 1830s, when beaver-skin hats were fashionable with European gentlemen. In 1825, William Ashley established an annual rendezvous of trappers. (Rendezvous is the French word for "meeting.") At these gatherings, ammunition, food, and other supplies were traded for furs. The rendezvous also provided an important chance for trappers to exchange news and enjoy each other's company.

In 1832, a trapping and trading party of more than one hundred men, led by Captain Benjamin L. E. de Bonneville, came to Wyoming. In 1833, Bonneville's group discovered an oil

▼ More than five thousand explorers, soldiers, and settlers carved their names on Independence Rock near Casper.

spring in the Wind River Basin. A year later, traders William Sublette and Robert Campbell built eastern Wyoming's Fort William, which was later renamed Fort Laramie. The fort was the region's first permanent trading post.

Nine years later, in 1842, the famous scout and trapper Jim Bridger and his partner Louis Vasquez founded Fort Bridger in southwestern Wyoming. Once these trading posts were established, the rendezvous became less important. Also, extensive trapping had reduced beaver populations almost to extinction by the 1840s. When the beavers nearly died out, so did the fashion for beaver hats.

Wyoming then became important as a path to points further west. The desire for land and gold led to a wave of westward travel in the 1840s. Explorers found new trails through Wyoming, including the Oregon Trail, which cut through the Rocky Mountains at South Pass. By the mid-1840s, pioneers streamed along three Wyoming trails that all crossed South Pass. The Oregon Trail turned northwest. The California Trail split from the Oregon Trail in Idaho and went southwest. The Mormon Trail turned southwest at Fort Bridger, taking the followers of Mormon religious leader Brigham Young to Utah.

In 1842 and 1843, Lieutenant John C. Frémont explored the Wind River Mountains with a party of men guided by renowned scout Kit Carson. Frémont's report persuaded the U.S. Congress to vote in 1846 to establish forts along the

▼ A Union Pacific train pulls into Sherman Station, Wyoming Territory, in 1869.

Oregon Trail to protect settlers on their way west. Forts like Fort Phil Kearny were built along the wagon-train trails.

When the first settlers began crossing the Great Plains, Plains Indians often helped wagon trains find grazing land and water. But tribes gradually grew alarmed by the number of settlers who killed and frightened off game, brought diseases, and through carelessness set fires on the prairie. When fighting broke out, U.S. Army soldiers were sent to protect the settlers and prospectors.

The Indian Wars

During the Civil War, gold was discovered in Montana, causing a new flurry of westward travel. In 1863, the Bozeman Trail was blazed through northeastern Wyoming, cutting across Native American hunting grounds. Tribes realized that treaties were not going to protect their land, so they increased their attacks on troops and settlers. One of the major battles of the Indian wars, known as the Fetterman Massacre, occurred in 1866 near Fort Kearny. Sioux warriors led by Crazy Horse and Red Cloud attacked and killed Lt. Colonel W. J. Fetterman and all eighty of his men. The following year, Captain James Powell drove back more than a thousand Sioux during the Wagon Box fight. Powell's forces possessed new repeating rifles that shifted the balance in favor of the army.

In 1868, the Sioux were forced to sign a treaty giving up much of their land. In return, the army agreed to give up Fort Phil Kearny and two other forts and to leave northeastern Wyoming to the Native Americans.

No major problems erupted until 1874, when prospectors found gold just east of Wyoming in the Black Hills of South Dakota. Despite the treaty, miners poured into the area, which the Sioux considered sacred.

Perhaps the most devastating thing whites did to the tribes was hunt the buffalo, their chief source of food, clothing, and shelter, to near

Esther Hobart Morris

In 1869, the men of Carter County were choosing their representative to the first Wyoming legislature. Esther Morris invited twenty leading citizens, including the Democratic and Republican candidates, to tea. Morris was already a good friend of the Democrat, Colonel William H. Bright, because she had cared for his wife during the birth of their child. She persuaded Bright to support a woman's suffrage bill if elected; the Republican also agreed. When Bright was elected, he kept his promise, and for the first time anywhere in the world, women were granted the right to vote!

The following year, Esther Morris became the first woman in the country elected justice of the peace. On the day of her swearing in, her husband John made a scene in the courtroom. Esther fined him for contempt of court. When John refused to pay, Esther sent him to jail. The dispute was typical of Morris. An attorney who practiced before her court said, "She showed no mercy, but her decisions were always fair."

extinction. Only twenty-five lonely specimens of the 75 million bison previously alive survived in Yellowstone by 1905. William F. Cody became known as Buffalo Bill because he skillfully hunted buffalo to feed hungry crews working on the railroad being built to cross the country. Cody later regretted his participation in the buffalo slaughter.

In 1867, the Union Pacific Railroad brought permanent settlements to the Wyoming Territory. Cities like Cheyenne, Laramie, and Green River sprang up along its tracks. Although they started as mere clusters of tents, these cities boomed as people scrambled west to seize their chance at riches — or at least a piece of land to call their own. Newcomers often worked for the railroad, opened stores, or ran other services like restaurants, laundries, and blacksmith shops to support the territory's growing mining and cattle industries.

A Vote for Justice
On December 10, 1869, the territorial legislature of Wyoming

▼ North American bison (buffalo) were hunted almost to extinction by expert sharpshooters as depicted in this painting of a buffalo and elk hunt in the 1880s.

This wood engraving shows women at the Cheyenne polls casting their ballots in a local election in Wyoming in 1870. This was fifty years before the Nineteenth Amendment to the U.S. Constitution, giving women the right to vote, was passed in 1920.

earned a place in history by granting women the right to vote, hold office, and serve on juries. At the time, women were not allowed to vote in any other state or country. When the bill passed, it was international news. Women from England cabled their congratulations. The King of Prussia sent word to President Ulysses S. Grant that the bill showed "evidence of progress and enlightenment and civil liberty in America."

By granting women the right to vote, Wyoming also hoped to increase the number of women moving there. Lonely miners, railroad workers, and cowboys outnumbered the territory's women six to one.

Not only did Wyoming's men need female companionship, but they also sought what they hoped would be the civilizing influence of women. The young territory had a serious crime problem. When the Union Pacific finished building its rails, thousands of out-of-work railroad men filled the streets of Laramie, joining cowboys and miners in rowdy brawls. Vigilante justice, in which armed mobs ruled with rope and gun, was unfair and often led to more lawlessness. When men arrested for murder or for stealing cattle or horses were brought to trial, all-male juries often set them free out of sympathy for a fellow in trouble. People hoped that women serving on juries might bring law and order to the area.

Brief as a Sunset

Although cowboys have created a lasting impression in the minds of people throughout the world, their way of life lasted barely one generation. From the end of the Civil War (1865) to the mid-1880s, about forty thousand cowboys rode the cattle trails across the Great Plains. The Age of the Cowboy ended because of a combination of bad weather, low cattle prices, and advances in railroad transportation between ranches and meat-processing plants.

Reporters from all over the world covered the first trials in which women served on juries, often with a mocking tone. But Wyomingites found that women could indeed help tame the Wild West.

Wyoming was so pleased with its decision to grant women rights that the legislature refused to repeal the law when the U.S. Congress suggested that such repeal might be a condition for earning statehood. Wyoming entered the union on July 10, 1890, becoming the forty-fourth state. Wyoming women retained their rights.

▲ Wagon ruts are still visible along the route of the Oregon Trail where it passed through Wyoming.

A Great Injustice

The railroad brought both progress and problems to Wyoming. Steam engines hungry for coal fueled the mining industry. The Union Pacific ran its own coal mines, using local labor. Working conditions in the mines were very poor, and the pay was low. When the miners went on strike in 1875, the railroad hired new workers from China. The railroad hired the Chinese because they knew the Chinese would not join miners' unions or strike for higher wages. Instead of blaming Union Pacific, many local miners blamed the Chinese for the failed strike and the loss of their jobs.

In 1885, near Rock Springs, where 331 Chinese and 150 white miners worked together, a fight between workers grew into a full-scale riot. The angry mob killed twenty-eight Chinese miners and hurt fifteen more. Chinese homes were torched. Hundreds of Asians were threatened and harassed into leaving.

Wyoming's governor, Francis E. Warren, condemned what became known as the Rock Springs Massacre as "the most damnable and brutal outrage that ever occurred in any country." However, the state's grand jury would not charge any of the sixteen men arrested for taking part in the massacre, so they were never brought to trial. Instead, most of the state's Chinese population fled.

The Range Wars

Wyoming's crime problem took a new form in the 1890s. Cattle and sheep ranchers got into violent disputes over who had the right to graze the open range. As more settlers

DID YOU KNOW?

Intense battle during the Johnson County War was avoided by the use of the telegraph. One man was killed and a house was set on fire by Texas gunmen hired by cattle barons. Before the small ranchers who had been gathering an army of their own could take their revenge, federal troops arrived, summoned by the telegraph. Cross-country telegraph lines were completed in 1861, thirty-one years before the Johnson County War.

moved into the new state, conflicts also arose between large cattle "barons" and small ranchers, who began building fences on the open range. The barons blamed their financial problems on the small ranchers and accused them of rustling (stealing) the barons' herds.

In 1892, some cattle barons hired a group of Texas gunmen to kill people on a list of suspected rustlers in Johnson County. When two allies of the accused small ranchers were killed, neighbors of the slain ranchers took up arms. They would have killed the gunmen if U.S. soldiers had not arrived. Cattle barons continued to use masked gunmen to threaten sheep ranchers, shooting and even dynamiting flocks, and occasionally killing shepherds, too. In 1909, seven cattlemen were arrested for the murder of three sheep ranchers, and the violence died down.

Booms and Busts

In its first twenty years of statehood, Wyoming's economy and population boomed. Coal and oil became big business. By World War I (1917–1918), the state had become a major oil producer — but coal, oil, and livestock prices all fell in the 1920s. A combination of droughts, miners' strikes, and competition from other oil-producing states caused Wyoming's economy to crash, even before the Great Depression. In the ten years before the Depression, the majority of the state's banks went out of business. Only federal assistance kept Wyoming's economy from utter collapse, and the worldwide Depression just made hard times worse.

During World War II (1941–1945), the country needed Wyoming's coal, oil, lumber, and cattle products. Discovery of large uranium deposits and the building of Francis E. Warren Air Force Base gave Wyoming an additional postwar boost.

The Heartless History of Heart Mountain

In 1942, almost 120,000 Japanese Americans were forced from their homes in California, Oregon, Washington, and Arizona and sent to relocation centers like Wyoming's Heart Mountain camp. This was the single largest forced relocation in U.S. history. Two-thirds of these people were American citizens. The bombing of Pearl Harbor was the excuse given for the internment of these Americans. Japanese-American families were given one week to conclude their business, and they could pack only what they could carry. The Heart Mountain camp was primitive, cold, and cramped. Many Japanese Americans spent three years in camps like Heart Mountain. In 1988, Congress issued a formal apology and paid compensation to victims of this misguided wartime policy.

◄ Japanese Americans were forced to live in rows of barracks and inhospitable surroundings in the Heart Mountain Internment Camp.

Just Passing Through

> [A cowboy] was out fixing his fence one day when a tourist lady pulled up. "Young man," she said, "I understand you have more cows than you do people out here. Why is that?" He looked at her with a steady gaze, hooked his thumb in his belt, and replied, "We prefer 'em."
>
> — *Former U.S. Senator Alan Simpson,*
> *in a speech about the Brady Bill, 1994*

Millions of people have crossed Wyoming, but few have stayed. For many years, settlers traveled through the state on their way to Montana, California, and other western destinations. Today millions visit Wyoming's natural wonders, then return to their homes in more populated areas. Between 1970 and 1980, a boom in Wyoming's mining industry led to one of the highest population growth rates in the country (about 41 percent). When oil, coal, and uranium prices fell in the 1980s, unemployed workers left the state. According to the 1980 U.S. census, the only state with fewer people than Wyoming was Alaska. By 1990, Alaska's population had

Age Distribution in Wyoming
(2000 Census)

Age	Population
0–4	30,940
5–19	114,406
20–24	33,455
25–44	138,619
45–64	118,669
65 & over	57,693

Patterns of Immigration

The total number of people who immigrated to Wyoming in 1998 was 159. Of that number, the largest immigrant groups were from Mexico (26.4%), India (9.4%), and the People's Republic of China (6.3%).

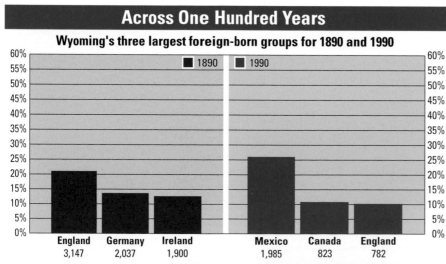

Across One Hundred Years

Wyoming's three largest foreign-born groups for 1890 and 1990

■ 1890   ■ 1990

| England 3,147 | Germany 2,037 | Ireland 1,900 | Mexico 1,985 | Canada 823 | England 782 |

Total state population: 60,705
Total foreign-born: 14,913 (24.6%)

Total state population: 453,588
Total foreign-born: 7,647 (1.7%)

▶ The Yellowstone Drug Store in Shoshoni (population about 500) is considered to be centrally located by Wyomingites. It is only 22 miles (35 km) from Riverton, 180 miles (290 km) from Yellowstone National Park, and 380 miles (611 km) from Denver, Colorado.

grown enough to leave Wyoming with the fewest people of any state in the union. Wyoming's average of approximately 5 people per square mile (2 people per sq km) is well below the national average of 80 people per square mile (31 people per sq km). About half of Wyoming's people live in the southeastern corner of the state.

In 1868, the transcontinental railroad crossed Wyoming Territory; many towns like Cheyenne were built along its route. Some towns started out as railroad workers' camps; some grew out of former military forts. The cattle, oil, and mining industries created more towns. Later, tourist attractions like Grand Teton and Yellowstone National Parks inspired the growth of cities like Jackson and Cody.

Approximately two-thirds of Wyomingites live in urban areas, although the cities are small. Some Wyoming towns consist of just a few buildings along a main road: fast food

DID YOU KNOW?

Treasure hunters still come to Wyoming looking for legendary loot. They comb Wyoming's mountains for the Lost Cabin mine, and scan the wilds of Slade's Canyon and Castle Creek for loot supposedly hidden by desperadoes like the James Boys, Teton Jackson, and Butch Cassidy.

Heritage and Background, Wyoming   Year 2000

▶ Here is a look at the racial backgrounds of Wyomingites today. Wyoming ranks forty-third among all U.S. states with regard to African Americans as a percentage of the population.

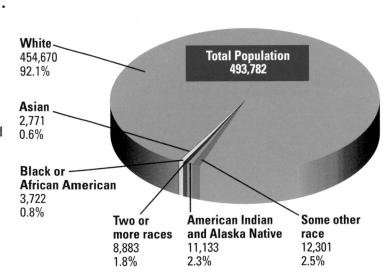

Total Population 493,782

White
454,670
92.1%

Asian
2,771
0.6%

Black or African American
3,722
0.8%

Native Hawaiian and Other Pacific Islander
302
0.1%

Two or more races
8,883
1.8%

American Indian and Alaska Native
11,133
2.3%

Some other race
12,301
2.5%

Note: 6.4% (31,669) of the population identify themselves as **Hispanic or Latino,** a cultural designation that crosses racial lines. Hispanics and Latinos are counted in this category as well as the racial category of their choice.

chains, gas stations, car dealers, and trailer parks. Ghost towns, where nature rapidly swallows the signs of civilization, are scattered throughout the state. Wild animals live in the empty buildings and weeds break up pavement. Most of these ghost towns were built near mines that were depleted.

Wyoming has become a popular destination for people moving in search of peaceful natural surroundings. Further attractions include no income tax, a low cost of living, and a near absence of crime. For the luxury of elbowroom under clear, sunny skies, newcomers will gladly endure the isolation and harsh weather.

Educational Levels of Wyoming Workers (age 25 and over)

Less than 9th grade	10,614
9th to 12th grade, no diploma	27,703
High school graduate, including equivalency	97,779
Some college, no degree or associate degree	110,405
Bachelor's degree	47,066
Graduate or professional degree	22,096

▼ Surrounded by majestic mountains, pristine lakes, and flowing streams, Dubois attracts full-time residents and vacationers from across the United States.

Ethnicity and Religion

Immigrants came to Wyoming from England, Germany, Scandinavia, China, Russia, Italy, Greece, and Ireland. Today, almost all of Wyoming's citizens (about 98 percent) were born in the United States. Most in-migrants (new residents coming from within the United States) come from Nebraska and Colorado. The majority of out-migrants move to California and Colorado. More than eleven thousand Native Americans call Wyoming home. Over half are Shoshone and Northern Arapahos living on the Wind River Indian Reservation, the state's only reservation.

The largest religious groups in Wyoming are various Protestant denominations: Baptist, Congregationalist, Episcopalian, Lutheran, Methodist, and Presbyterian. Most other residents are Roman Catholics and Mormons.

▲ Bighorn, Medicine Wheel National Monument.

Education

Wyoming's first school was founded at Fort Laramie by the fort's chaplain in 1852. In 1869, the territorial legislature passed a law providing for a tax to support schools. District schools sprang up in many communities. Young Wyomingites are required to attend school from age seven to sixteen or until they complete the eighth grade.

Only Alaska spends more money per pupil than Wyoming. Both states must contend with small, scattered communities spread out over vast distances. In some Wyoming towns, winter roads are impassable, so the state may pay for apartments that allow teachers to live within walking distance of the school. Some Wyoming children travel 75 miles (121 km) each way to school.

Wyoming has only one four-year university, the University of Wyoming at Laramie, established in 1886. It offers many fields of study, including agriculture, arts and sciences, commerce and industry, education, engineering, law, nursing, and pharmacy. The university also has a graduate school. Casper, Cheyenne, Powell, Riverton, Rock Springs, Sheridan, and Torrington all have two-year community colleges.

Small Schools Breed Readers

Wyoming has one of the highest percentages of people who can read and write in the United States. This may be due to the very low student-teacher ratio in this least-populated state. In many isolated areas, children in kindergarten through eighth grade attend one-teacher schools. With classes this small and teachers so familiar with each student, there is little chance to hide in the back of the room just pretending to read.

High and Dry

> If summer falls on a weekend, let's have a picnic.
> — *An early settler's joke,*
> *based on Wyoming's short summers*

Wyoming is higher than every other state except Colorado. Thanks to an average elevation of 6,700 feet (2,042 meters), the state has cool, dry weather. The average yearly rainfall is only 14.5 inches (37 centimeters), most of which falls in the mountains. Snow dusts the grasslands but dumps on the mountains. Some places in the Tetons and Yellowstone National Park receive an average of almost 22 feet (7 m) of snow each year!

The only state colder than Wyoming is Alaska. In the highlands, temperatures fall below freezing year-round. Wyoming's summers are beautiful but short, a time to work hard on ranches and farms, and to enjoy.

Plains, Mountains, and Basins
Wyoming forms a rough rectangle within a group of states in the west called the Mountain States. Their majestic purple mountains formed when the land lifted and folded 65 million years ago. Wyoming's land is divided into three major areas: the Great Plains, the Rocky Mountains, and the Intermontane Basins. The Great Plains, which stretch

Highest Point
Gannett Peak
13,804 feet (4,207 m) above sea level.

▼ *From left to right:* **Bison mother and calf; storm clouds on the Beartooth Highway; a black-footed ferret; Yellowstone Falls; Old Trail Town, Cody; Jackson Hole ski resort.**

from Canada to Mexico, include part of eastern Wyoming, mostly covered by short-grass prairie used for grazing livestock. About one-third of the famous Black Hills lie in northeastern Wyoming; the rest are in South Dakota. To many Native Americans, these small mountains covered with dense pine forests are sacred land.

Ranges of the Rocky Mountain system radiate from Wyoming's northwest corner, including the Teton Range along the western border; the Wind River range stretching southeast from the Yellowstone Plateau; the Bighorn Mountains in the north-central area; and the Laramie Mountains in the southeast.

Intermontane means "between mountains." This region includes some fairly flat, mostly treeless areas between the mountains with short grasses and other low plants good for grazing. The Intermontane region includes most of south-central Wyoming. It is also known as the Wyoming Basin.

The Divide and the Desert

Water from Wyoming's mountains flows into rivers, which eventually drain into the ocean. The Continental Divide separates those that drain into the Atlantic from those that drain into the Pacific. The Divide zigzags through Wyoming's highlands.

The Great Divide Basin in south-central Wyoming does not drain at all, but receives very little rain. The nearby Killpecker Sand Dunes contain the largest active sand dunes outside of the Sahara Desert. "Active" dunes are blown along by the wind.

Lakes and Rivers

Three great river systems start in Wyoming's mountains — the Missouri, Colorado, and Columbia. Water rushing through narrow gaps between rocks carves steep canyons

---

Average January temperature
Casper: 24°F (-5°C)
Cheyenne:
   27°F (-3°C)

Average July temperature
Casper: 71°F (22°C)
Cheyenne:
   70°F (21°C)

Average yearly rainfall
Casper:
   11.4 inches (29 cm)
Cheyenne:
   13.3 inches (34 cm)

Average yearly snowfall
Casper:
   80.5 inches (205 cm)
Cheyenne:
   52.1 inches (132 cm)

DID YOU KNOW?

The pronghorn antelope, native to Wyoming, is the fastest animal in North America. It can run 60 miles (97 km) per hour. Only the cheetah is faster.

Largest Lakes

Yellowstone Lake
88,000 acres
   (35,614 hectares)

Jackson Lake
25,540 acres (10,336 ha)

Fremont Lake
4,996 acres (2,022 ha)

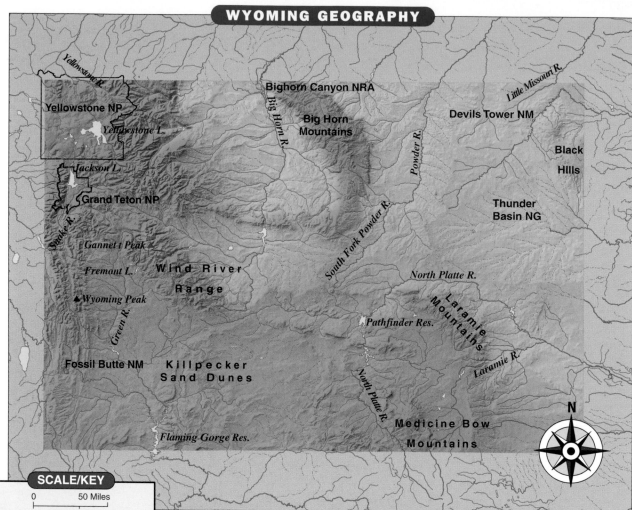

Yellowstone R.

Little Missouri R.

Yellowstone NP

Bighorn Canyon NRA

Devils Tower NM

Yellowstone L.

Big Horn Mountains

Big Horn R.

Powder R.

Black Hills

Jackson L.

Grand Teton NP

Thunder Basin NG

Snake R.

South Fork Powder R.

Gannet t Peak

North Platte R.

Fremont L.

Wind River Range

Laramie Mountains

Wyoming Peak

Pathfinder Res.

Green R.

Fossil Butte NM

Killpecker Sand Dunes

North Platte R.

Laramie R.

N

Flaming Gorge Res.

Medicine Bow Mountains

SCALE/KEY

0	50 Miles
0	50 Kilometers

NP	National Park
NG	National Grassland
NM	National Monument
NRA	National Recreation Area
▲	Highest Point
▲	Important Peaks
	Mountains

and creates dazzling waterfalls. At 308 feet (94 m), the Lower Falls at Yellowstone National Park are twice the height of New York's Niagara Falls.

Hundreds of lakes glitter like blue jewels in Wyoming's mountain ranges. The water is very pure and very cold. The state's creeks and streams vary with the seasons. They are swollen with melted snow in spring, but some dry up completely by summer's end. Rock dust clouds the streams that feed the lakes. Centuries ago, when glaciers slowly crawled over the state's landscape, the giant sheets of ice scoured rocks and mountains, creating the rock dust. When these particles reach the mountain lakes, the water is tinted brilliant blue and green hues.

Plants and Animals

Wyoming provides many different kinds of habitats for a wide variety of animal and plant species. Large mammals abound in Wyoming. Some of the largest species in North America live under the state's spacious skies. America's largest remaining herds of bison and bighorn sheep can be found on Wyoming's plains and mountains.

North America's most endangered mammal, the rare black-footed ferret, lives only in Wyoming. Other endangered species also live in the wilds of Wyoming. These include the American peregrine falcon, bald eagle, gray wolf, grizzly bear, and Wyoming toad.

Wyoming's lakes and rivers share the diversity of species. The bright blue waters are home to seven kinds of trout, as well as bass, catfish, and salmon. Ospreys, ducks, trumpeter swans, white pelicans, and wild turkeys are just a few of the birds that fly over the state's mountains and plains.

About 2.7 million acres (1.1 million ha) of Wyoming are set aside for parks and preserves. Forests cover nearly one-sixth of the state's land, about 10 million acres (4 million ha), mostly in the mountains.

The state's wild plants include arnica, bluegrass, buttercup, cactus, evening star, five-finger, flax, forget-me-not, goldenrod, redtop, sagebrush, wheatgrass, and windflower. Over 150 types of grass are native to Wyoming. Many of these species are found in the Thunder Basin National Grassland in the northeast corner of the state.

Major Rivers

Green River
730 miles (1,175 km)

Yellowstone River
682 miles (1,097 km)

North Platte River
618 miles (994 km)

▼ Devils Tower is a huge volcanic rock that rises 867 feet (264 m) above northeastern Wyoming's grasslands. This spectacular rock was made even more famous by the 1977 movie *Close Encounters of the Third Kind*, in which it was the secret base of alien visitors.

Cattle and Coal

> The best things in life are free.
>
> — *1920s song written by Buddy DeSylva,*
> *Lew Brown, and Ray Henderson*

Wyoming's first industry was fur. But when the fashion for beaver-skin hats declined with beaver populations, Wyomingites started selling supplies to travelers heading west on wagon trains. When the railroad reached Wyoming in 1867, the cattle industry boomed. Ranchers who grazed their herds on the state's vast grasslands could now easily ship their meat to market. The railroad also boosted Wyoming's growing mining and tourist industries.

Livestock, Farms, and Forestry

Cattle ranching is Wyoming's biggest agricultural business. Livestock and livestock products account for over 80 percent of the state's farm income. There are about 850,000 sheep and 1.3 million cattle in the state — roughly five cows for every two people! Wyoming is a national leader in the production of sheep and wool.

Wyoming's climate is too dry to support much farming. But the state grows beans, sugar beets, and wheat, plus grain and hay to feed livestock. The chief commercial tree species are Douglas fir, Engelmann spruce, lodgepole pine, and ponderosa pine. Aspen and yellow pine are also harvested.

Mining and Manufacturing

Wyoming derives a larger part of its income from mining than any other state. It produces the most coal and is a national leader in petroleum and natural gas. Oil and gas wells are almost as common as cattle. Wyoming sells electricity to other states. The twenty-four-story Jim Bridger Power Plant, near Rock Springs, burns coal to

Top Employers
(of workers age sixteen and over)
Services 41.9%
Wholesale and retail trade 14.1%
Agriculture, forestry, fisheries, and mining 10.7%
Construction 8.7%
Transportation, communications, and other public utilities 6.6%
Federal, state, and local government (including military) 6.3%
Manufacturing . . . 4.9%
Finance, insurance, and real estate 4.7%

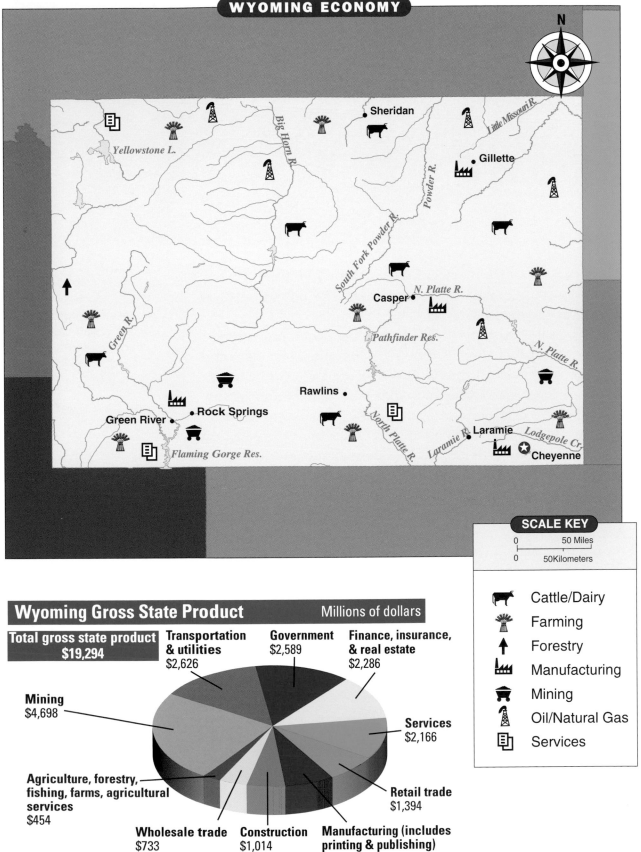

Map labels:

Yellowstone L.
Sheridan
Gillette
Little Missouri R.
Big Horn R.
Powder R.
South Fork Powder R.
Casper
N. Platte R.
Pathfinder Res.
N. Platte R.
Green R.
Rawlins
North Platte R.
Rock Springs
Green River
Flaming Gorge Res.
Laramie
Lodgepole Cr.
Cheyenne
Laramie R.

SCALE KEY

0 — 50 Miles
0 — 50 Kilometers

- Cattle/Dairy
- Farming
- Forestry
- Manufacturing
- Mining
- Oil/Natural Gas
- Services

Wyoming Gross State Product
Millions of dollars

Total gross state product $19,294

Transportation & utilities $2,626

Government $2,589

Finance, insurance, & real estate $2,286

Mining $4,698

Services $2,166

Agriculture, forestry, fishing, farms, agricultural services $454

Retail trade $1,394

Wholesale trade $733

Construction $1,014

Manufacturing (includes printing & publishing) $1,333

produce four times more electricity than Wyoming needs, and the rest is bought by other states. The power plant is Wyoming's tallest building.

Wyoming is also a source for two chemicals that many people use in their homes all the time: trona (soda ash) and bentonite. Almost all the natural trona in the world can be found in the state. Trona is used as baking soda and in the manufacture of paper, glass, steel, and iron. Bentonite is a special kind of clay that can absorb fifteen times its volume in water. Glue, paint, detergent, polish, makeup, toothpaste, and cat litter all contain bentonite.

Large deposits of uranium were found in the Powder River area in 1951 and later in many other parts of Wyoming. By the late 1950s, the state ranked third among those with known reserves of this element, which is used in nuclear power plants and weapons.

Manufacturing makes up a smaller portion of Wyoming's gross state product than in most states. There are very few factories in the state. Most of Wyoming's manufacturing relates to its natural resources, such as refining petroleum and making products from food, wood, stone, clay, and glass. The state also manufactures some machinery and printed materials.

Services, Transportation, and Tourism

The service industries make up the biggest part of Wyoming's gross state product. Government services like public schools, hospitals, and military bases employ more Wyomingites than any other economic activity.

The service industries also include communications

▲ Today's cowboys and cowgirls herd cattle in much the same way their predecessors did in the 1800s.

Mighty Missiles

In 1958, the nation's first intercontinental ballistic missile (ICBM) site brought defense industry jobs to Wyoming. F.E. Warren Air Force Base outside Cheyenne contains most of the nation's ICBMs. Each nuclear warhead can destroy a city after launch from its underground silo. Since most Wyomingites are pro-military, there have been few protests against the ICBMs. In fact, Mayor Worth Story declared at the base's opening, "Cheyenne is proud to be the nation's #1 target for enemy missiles."

(telephone companies), utilities (electricity, gas, and water), and transportation. Pipeline companies, which carry Wyoming's oil and gas to processing and distributing sites, are a major part of the transportation industry, as are the railroads, which move products from Wyoming's mines and farms.

There has been no passenger train service in Wyoming since 1983. The state has about 39,000 miles (63,000 km) of roads and highways. Wyoming has the nation's highest rate of motor vehicle ownership, but also one of the highest rates of traffic deaths. Wyoming's leading retail businesses are car dealerships, grocery stores, and restaurants.

Wyoming bulges with tourists in the summer and ski seasons. An estimated seven million people visit the state each year. During peak seasons, tourists outnumber natives roughly fourteen to one. The tourist industry employs Wyomingites at hotels, motels, dude ranches, ski resorts, and restaurants, and as park rangers and tour guides.

▲ Mining is Wyoming's largest industry. Pictured here, an aerial view of Exxon's coal mine in Gillette.

The Future

Wyoming's economy has gone up and down with changes in cattle, coal, oil, and uranium prices. Wyoming's leaders are trying to broaden the state's economy. But without facilities like factories or industrial parks, and with few large cities full of professionals and skilled workers, the state is finding it difficult to attract new businesses. Still, despite an average income $4,000 lower than the national average, there is not much poverty in Wyoming. The cost of living is relatively low, and it is one of the few states in the union with no income tax. And the best things about Wyoming are free.

Made in Wyoming

Leading farm products and crops
Cattle
Hay
Sugar beets
Barley
Sheep, lambs
Milk
Wheat
Hogs
Beans
Oats

Other products
Coal and oil products
Natural gas
Chemicals
Industrial machinery and equiptment
Lumber and wood products
Stone, clay, and glass products

Major Airports		
Airport	Location	Passengers per year (2000)
Jackson Hole Airport	Jackson	362,360
Natrona County International	Casper	139,674
Yellowstone Regional Airport	Cody	60,580

Don't Fence Me In

> In the Cowboy State, gun control simply means how steady you hold your rifle.
>
> — *Former Senator Alan Simpson, during a discussion of the Brady Bill, which passed in 1993*

Wyomingites favor minimal government interference with their freedom. As the above quote suggests, most oppose gun control. Citizens of the Cowboy State tend to be conservative and Republican. They think government should be barely seen and infrequently heard.

The state is governed by the same constitution that was adopted in 1890, when Wyoming became a state. However, this constitution has been amended many times. Amendments (changes) to the state constitution are proposed by the legislature, then voted on by the people. To become law, an amendment must win a majority in a general election. Like the federal government, Wyoming's government is divided into three branches: the executive, the legislative, and the judicial.

The Executive Branch

The governor, who heads the executive branch, is elected by the people to a four-year term. In 1992, Wyomingites voted to set term limits for many elected officials; as a result, no one person can be governor more than twice in a sixteen-year period.

The governor votes to approve or veto new laws passed by the state legislature and also appoints certain state officials, like the attorney general and the heads of the state budget and personnel departments. Voters elect four other officials to the executive branch: the secretary of state, auditor, treasurer, and superintendent of public instruction. Wyoming does not have a lieutenant governor. If the governor dies or resigns, the secretary of state steps in until a new governor is elected.

State Constitution

"**A**ll power is inherent in the people, and all free governments are founded on their authority, and instituted for their peace, safety and happiness; for the advancement of these ends they have at all times an inalienable and indefeasible right to alter, reform or abolish the government in such manner as they may think proper."

— *Preamble to the 1890 Wyoming State Constitution*

Elected Posts in the Executive Branch

Office	Length of Term	Term Limits
Governor	4 years	2 consecutive terms in a 16-year period
Secretary of State	4 years	none
Superintendent of Public Instruction	4 years	2 consecutive terms
Treasurer	4 years	none
Auditor	4 years	none

The Legislative Branch

Wyoming has a thirty-member senate and a sixty-member house of representatives. The legislators discuss and vote on proposed new laws and suggested changes to old ones. They meet every January for a maximum of forty days in any given year and no more than sixty days in each two-year period. These sessions are shorter than in most other states, demonstrating Wyoming's wish to keep government to a minimum. If needed, the governor may call for special legislative sessions.

The Judicial Branch

The highest court in the state consists of five supreme court justices. Their job is to clarify any vague laws and decide whether any laws violate Wyoming's constitution. They also hear appeals from the lower courts.

Most major trials are held in one of the state's nine district courts. The governor appoints one or two district judges to each of these courts for a six-year term. The governor appoints the supreme court justices for eight-year terms, choosing from nominees selected by the Wyoming Judicial Nominating Commission. At the next election, the citizens vote

▼ Wyoming's capitol building in Cheyenne was completed just in time for statehood in 1890, although two wings were finished later.

on whether or not to let the appointed judges remain in office. Wyoming also has circuit courts, police courts, municipal courts, and justice-of-the-peace courts.

National and Local Government

Like all the other states in the union, Wyoming sends two senators to Washington to represent it in the federal government. Because of its small population, Wyoming sends only one representative to the U.S. House of Representatives and has only three votes in the Electoral College, which determines the outcome of presidential elections.

The Equality State has elected quite a few women to serve in public office. In 1955, Wyoming's legislature chose Esther Hobart Morris to represent the state in Statuary Hall in the Capitol building in Washington, D.C.

From 1930–2000, Wyoming elected sixteen women to the position of state senator. From 1910–2000, 71 women were elected to Wyoming's house of representatives. Of those 71 women, two became Speaker of the House.

Wyoming has twenty-three counties and ninety-seven incorporated cities and towns. A three-member board of commissioners governs each county. Most cities are led by a mayor and council.

Wyoming Politics

Since 1890, Republicans have won two-thirds of state and local elections. The cities in southern Wyoming have traditionally been more Democratic, while the rural counties in the north tend to vote Republican. Wyomingites have voted for twice as many Republicans as Democrats in presidential elections.

Government plays an unusually important role in Wyoming's economy because the federal government owns half the state's land. Federal agencies control any grazing,

Legislative Branch			
House	**Number of Members**	**Length of Term**	**Term Limits**
Senate	30 senators	4 years	No more than 3 terms in a 24-year period
House of Representatives	60 representatives	2 years	No more than 6 terms in a 24-year period

logging, and mining that takes place on government land, as well as the administration of Wyoming's national forests, parks, Indian reservation, and other public lands.

In 1995, Wyoming's government proved it had the wisdom to change with the times. In the early 1900s, ranchers persuaded the federal government to put a bounty on wolves, because packs sometimes ate cattle and sheep. Within twenty years, Wyoming's wolves were gone. Environmentalists in the 1990s correctly predicted that wolves could be brought back to Yellowstone National Park without endangering herds. In 1995, three wolf packs from Canada were released in Yellowstone. Wolves have thrived in the park ever since!

Taxes and Government Spending

Money for government programs is hard to come by in the Cowboy State, because unlike most states, Wyoming does not have a state income tax. However, the state credits its very low crime rate to the fact that it spends more than the national average on crime prevention and police. Since the 1970s, the state legislature has taxed minerals and other resources to fund such spending and finance public schools, roads, aid to the poor, and wildlife management.

<aside>

A Wyomingite Vice President

Richard B. Cheney (2000–2004)

Richard B. Cheney was born in Lincoln, Nebraska, on January 30, 1941. He grew up in Casper, Wyoming, where he was captain of his high school football team and president of his senior class. He earned bachelor's and master's degrees in political science from the University of Wyoming.

Between 1969 and 1977, Cheney served in the administrations of Presidents Richard Nixon and Gerald Ford. In 1978, he was elected to represent Wyoming in the U.S. House of Representatives. Cheney was reelected five times. From March 1989 to January 1993, he served as Secretary of Defense under President George Bush (senior). For his leadership during the Gulf War, he was awarded the Presidential Medal of Freedom. Cheney then became chairman and CEO of the Halliburton company before becoming vice president to George W. Bush in 2000.

Cheney's hobbies include reading and fishing.

Left: Air Force Two, the plane used by Vice President Dick Cheney, sits on the tarmac in front of the Grand Tetons in Jackson, Wyoming.

</aside>

Wide-Open Wonderland

> Most of Wyoming's people enjoy a love affair with space.
>
> — *Robert Harold Brown,*
> *University of Wyoming geographer, in*
> *Wyoming: A Geography, 1980*

Wyoming's natural wonders and historic buildings reflect the state's rich history. From the fossils buried in its soil to the wagon-wheel ruts carved by settlers making their way across the Oregon Trail to the gushing geysers of Yellowstone National Park, Wyoming's landscape tells many tales.

Some of the best fossil beds in the world are at Fossil Butte National Monument near Kemmerer. It holds the fossil remains of fish and plants that lived in the sea that covered Wyoming about fifty million years ago. Other fossils include a 13-foot (4 m) crocodile and the oldest known bat, just two of the amazing exhibits at Fossil Butte. Southwestern Wyoming is especially rich in fossils. At many sites, visitors seeking hands-on experience are provided with professional tools and instructions about proper digging techniques. Guest diggers are allowed to keep any finds that are not considered rare.

Fort Laramie National Historic Site contains eleven buildings restored from the

◄ This statue in Douglas depicts the mythical "jackalope," used to tease city slickers unfamiliar with the state's real wildlife.

fort's glory days. Founded in 1834 by fur traders, the fort was bought by the U.S. military in 1849 as a base to protect settlers heading west on the Oregon Trail. Wyoming's oldest building is "Old Bedlam," a bunkhouse that earned its nickname by housing rowdy soldiers. In the summer, costumed guides give visitors a taste of military and civilian life at the fort, which later became a base of operations during the Indian wars and a major link for the Pony Express, the Overland Stage Line, and the transcontinental telegraph system.

Old Trail Town near Cody has a street lined with historic houses and buildings rescued from around the state. Tourists can visit the log cabin hideout of outlaws Butch Cassidy and the Sundance Kid. In Laramie, visitors see where Cassidy spent time behind bars at the Wyoming Territorial Prison. It was built in 1872 to house federal convicts. Also on the grounds are Frontier Town and the National U.S. Marshals Museum. The museum displays artifacts tracing two hundred years of law enforcement history. Frontier Town entertains visitors with a re-creation of the first trial in which women served as jurors, as well as with old-fashioned delights such as saloon-hall shows, melodramas, and puppet shows. Visitors who misbehave

▲ Buffalo Bill was one of the owners of the Sheridan Inn. He held auditions for his Wild West show from the hotel's elegant front porch. In 1965, the Sheridan was named a National Historic Landmark.

Impressive Prison

The Wyoming State Prison near Rawlins looks like a castle, since Gothic architecture was fashionable for public buildings of its era. Due to lack of funds, the castle took thirteen years to build and was completed in 1901. Five criminals met their end in the prison's gas chamber before the prison was converted to a museum in 1987. Bold tourists can even sit in the gas chamber's chair.

▲ The Wyoming State
Prison near Rawlins
is now a museum.

might just wind up in the Frontier Town Jail.

For a look at a more modern prison, tourists travel to
Rawlins, where the castle-like Wyoming State Prison
guarded criminals until 1982. Now the prison serves as a
tourist attraction, complete with frightening nighttime tours.

Libraries and Museums

Even before it became a state, Wyoming instituted the first
county public library system in the nation, in Laramie in
1886. Today, the state's principal libraries are located in
Cheyenne and at the University of Wyoming at Laramie.

Wyoming has about ninety museums, most featuring
pioneer and Native American relics. Some of the most
important are the State Museum and the Cheyenne Frontier
Days Old West Museum in Cheyenne; the Buffalo Bill
Historical Center and the Whitney Gallery of Western Art
in Cody; the Fort Bridger State Historical Site in Fort
Bridger; the Wyoming Pioneer Memorial Museum in
Douglas; and the National Museum of Wildlife Art in
Jackson.

Wyoming has many other fascinating museums. The
Riverton Museum displays Shoshone and Arapaho clothing

DID YOU KNOW?

Four in ten residents of
Riverton and Casper fish
frequently. These small
Wyoming towns have
a higher percentage of
anglers than most places
in the nation.

and offers demonstrations of silversmithing, quilting, and other pioneer skills. Buffalo's Jim Gatchell Memorial Museum offers an impressive collection of old photographs and Native American artifacts, plus cavalry tools and weapons from the days of the Indian wars. The Homesteaders Museum in Torrington houses a collection of artifacts of homestead life from the 1880s to the 1920s in a former Union Pacific depot. Sheridan's Bradford Brinton Memorial Museum and Historic Ranch has works by acclaimed American artists like Charles M. Russell and Frederic Remington.

To learn more about Wyoming's nonhuman residents, try the National Bighorn Sheep Interpretive Center in Dubois. Besides "Sheep Mountain," a model of bighorn habitat, the museum shows videos and has informative dioramas. The National Park Service operates the Fur Trade Museum at Moose, which covers every aspect of Wyoming's first industry.

Communications

Wyoming has about fifty newspapers, including five dailies. The largest papers are Casper's *Star-Tribune* and Cheyenne's *Wyoming Tribune-Eagle*. The state also produces about sixty periodicals.

▼ The interior of one of the buildings at Old Trail Town in Cody contains artifacts and furnishings from the late 1800s. Visitors can get an idea of what life was like in Wyoming more than a century ago.

Wyoming's first radio station started broadcasting out of Casper in 1930. The first television station went on the air from Cheyenne in 1954. Today, Wyoming has about sixty radio stations and ten TV stations. Several Wyoming communities now have cable television.

Music and Art

In keeping with their cowboy heritage, Wyomingites enjoy music. Jackson supports both the Grand Teton and the Grand Targhee Music Festivals. Shoshone hosts the State Championship Old-Time Fiddle Contest. Jackson also hosts the Jackson Hole Fall Arts Festival and the Mountain Artists' Fest Rendezvous. Crafts fans can visit Saratoga's Saratoga Craft Fair.

In recent years, cowboy poetry gatherings have cropped up all over the West, especially in Wyoming. The tradition dates back to the state's first settlers, who set their real-life adventures to rhyme and often to music. Today's cowboys write about many of the same joys and hardships experienced by their ancestors. These include the endless chores of fixing fences and gathering wayward cattle; the heart-warming companionship of loyal horses and dogs; and the camaraderie around the campfire. Cheyenne, Cody, Jackson, Kaycee, Laramie, Rawlins, Riverton, Rock Springs, and South Pass City are among the many towns that host festivals for cowboy poets.

Both Cheyenne and Casper support symphony orchestras. Casper also has its celebrated Casper Drum and Bugle Corps. The University of Wyoming at Laramie has a theater, and there are numerous other theaters throughout the state, including the Jackson Hole Playhouse, the Pink Garter Theater, and Dirty Jack's Wild West Theater & Opera House in Jackson; the Atlas Theater and Gertrude Krampert Summer Theatre in Casper; and the Variety Theatre in South Pass City.

▲ Actor Harrison Ford is one of Wyoming's most famous celebrities. He has played such popular movie roles as Han Solo (*Star Wars*), Indiana Jones (*Indiana Jones trilogy*), and the president of the United States (*Air Force One*).

Ride 'Em Cowboy!

Rodeo comes from the Spanish word *rodear* meaning to surround or round up. The first contests of rodeo skills were held between cowboys on the range, where they challenged each other in roping and riding to see who was the best hand. In 1872, Cheyenne hosted a limited competition, but large rodeos were not organized in Wyoming until the 1890s. The first rodeo to charge admission took place on July 4, 1888, in Prescott, Arizona. In 1897, Cheyenne's Frontier Day was criticized as a "roughneck show seeking to perpetuate the spirit of Western rowdyism." However, rodeos remain very popular throughout the West today.

For Fun

Rodeos are still a very popular form of entertainment in Wyoming. Cody and Cheyenne both claim to host the biggest and best rodeos. Small rodeos can be found all over the state.

Wyoming is too sparsely populated to support any professional sports teams. However, since 1999, it has had an indoor football team called the Cavalry, a member of the National Indoor Football League. The Casper Rockies are a farm team for the major league Colorado Rockies. Wyomingites are enthusiastic about their state's collegiate and high school teams.

Wyoming is also home to a variety of sporting events, including polo matches in Big Horn, bicycle and ski races, and hunting and fishing contests. The Jackson Hole Mountain Resort is among the finest in the world, and many Wyomingites enjoy both skiing and snowmobiling.

Solitude for Celebrities

Thanks to its small population and wide open spaces, Wyoming offers celebrities a chance to breathe free. Some famous faces prefer Wyoming's peace and quiet to the noise and crowds of Hollywood and New York City. In the 1980s, Harrison Ford built a ranch near Jackson. When he's in Wyoming, Ford likes to fish, hike, and ride horses.

▼ Garth Brooks, left, Charlie Daniels, center, and Chris LeDoux perform at the thirty-second Academy of Country Music Awards.

Wyoming Great

Chris LeDoux was sixteen when he achieved his childhood cowboy dream by winning the Little Britches World Championship for bareback bronco riding. LeDoux rode the rodeo circuit for several years after college, writing songs and selling cassettes of his music. After winning the World Championship for bareback bronco riding in 1976, LeDoux hung up his spurs in favor of pursuing music full time. He now tours with his band, the Western Underground, and has recorded about thirty albums to date.

Wonderful Wyomingites

Ladies and gentlemen,
permit us to introduce to you a Congress of
Rough Riders of the World!

*— Buffalo Bill Cody's opening address to audiences of his famous
Wild West exhibit, which toured from 1883 to 1913*

Following are a few of the thousands of people who were born, died, or spent much of their lives in Wyoming and made extraordinary contributions to the state and the nation.

JOHN COLTER
EXPLORER AND GUIDE
BORN: *c. 1775, near Staunton, VA*
DIED: *May 12, 1812, near New Haven, MO*

A fur trader and guide, Colter was part of the 1803–1806 Lewis and Clark Expedition, the first American exploration of lands acquired in the Louisiana Purchase. When Lewis and Clark were heading back east, Colter left the Expedition to investigate the still unexplored territory that is now Yellowstone National Park. Colter was the first white man to report on the region's amazing hot springs and geysers. His reports led to further explorations of Wyoming. In 1808, Colter was hunting with a group of Crow along the Missouri River when they met a large band of Blackfoot. In the ensuing battle, Colter was seen killing a Blackfoot. He was marked for death by the tribe. After an extremely narrow escape the next year, Colter moved near St. Louis and became a farmer.

SACAGAWEA
GUIDE
BORN: *c. 1788, Wyoming*
DIED: *1812*

As a young Shoshone girl, Sacagawea was captured by Hidatsa warriors and taken from her homelands. She later married a French trapper and lived in the Dakotas. Sacagawea met Lewis and Clark in 1805. She guided the explorers safely through Shoshone territory she had not seen since she was a child. Carrying her infant son on her back, Sacagawea led the explorers all the way to their goal, the Pacific Ocean.

JAMES BRIDGER
MOUNTAIN MAN

BORN: *March 17, 1804, Richmond, VA*
DIED: *July 17, 1881, near Kansas City, MO*

While still a teenager, Bridger took part in a trapping expedition that whetted his appetite for more adventures. At twenty-one, Bridger was probably the first white man to see Utah's Great Salt Lake. Trapping and trading in the wilderness led Bridger and some partners to build Fort Bridger near Wyoming's Green River. The fort became an important trading post and later a military post and Pony Express station.

CHIEF WASHAKIE
SHOSHONE CHIEF

BORN: *c. 1804*
DIED: *February 20, 1900, Fort Washakie*

In his youth, Washakie was a brave warrior, fighting against the Shoshones' enemies like the Blackfoot and Crow tribes. In the 1850s, Washakie and his people helped non-Native pioneers passing through their territory. Unlike many tribal leaders, Washakie understood that whites were not going to go away. Realizing that his people had a better chance of survival as farmers than as wandering hunters, he encouraged them to return to the agricultural lifestyle they had known before they became nomadic hunters on horseback. In 1868, Washakie negotiated the treaty that created the Wind River Indian Reservation, where Shoshones still live today. Washakie acted as a scout for the U.S. Army for twenty years during its campaigns against the Sioux, Cheyenne, and other tribes. Though he felt sad that his compromises had perhaps cost the Shoshones their freedom, Washakie helped preserve his tribe at a time when many other tribes were wiped out.

ESTHER HOBART MORRIS
JUSTICE OF THE PEACE

BORN: *August 8, 1814, Tioga County, NY*
DIED: *April 2, 1902, Cheyenne*

Born in New York State, Morris began supporting herself when she was orphaned at age eleven. She moved to Wyoming with her second husband, who was looking for gold. Morris has been called "the mother of woman suffrage in Wyoming" because of her important role in the passage of the territory's 1869 law granting women the right to vote. The following year, Morris was made the country's first female justice of the peace. Morris was considered tough but fair. None of the dozens of cases she tried was ever appealed.

JOHN MARION BOZEMAN
EXPLORER

BORN: *1835, Pickens County, GA*
DIED: *April 18, 1867, near the Yellowstone River*

Bozeman was born in Georgia, but

traveled west to the Colorado Territory. When he heard about a Montana gold strike in 1862, Bozeman tried to find a more direct route there. The result was the

Bozeman Trail through Wyoming, past the Bighorn Mountains. The U.S. Army soon fortified the trail as a way to help more settlers move west. However, because of successful Sioux attacks and the coming of the railroad, which offered a faster, safer passage west, the trail was abandoned by 1868. Bozeman was murdered under mysterious circumstances along the Yellowstone River, east of present-day Livingstone.

FRANCIS EMROY WARREN
POLITICIAN

BORN: *June 20, 1844, Hinsdale, MA*
DIED: *November 24, 1929, Washington, D.C.*

During the Civil War, Warren fought for the Union Army. He received the Congressional Medal of Honor for bravery under fire. In 1868, he moved to the Wyoming Territory, where he sold real estate, raised livestock, and promoted the first lighting system in Cheyenne. Warren entered local politics, and was elected mayor of Cheyenne in 1885. He went on to become the Wyoming Territory's governor, and then the state's first governor, before becoming one of Wyoming's first U.S. Senators. Warren served in the Senate until his death in 1929. The following year, Cheyenne's Fort D. A. Russell was renamed F. E. Warren Air Force Base in his honor.

WILLIAM FREDERICK "BUFFALO BILL" CODY
FRONTIERSMAN

BORN: *February 26, 1846, LeClair, IA*
DIED: *January 10, 1917, Denver, CO*

While still a teenager, Cody rode for the Pony Express. During the Civil War, he was a Union scout. Cody gained his nickname hunting buffalo to supply meat for crews working on the transcontinental railroad. He was Chief of Scouts for the Fifth U.S. Cavalry during the 1868–1872 Indian wars. Cody came to regret his part in the decimation of the buffalo herds and the Native American way of life. In 1883, he created a traveling entertainment called the Wild West. Cody refused to call the Wild West a "show," because it was as authentic as he could make it, featuring accurate scenes of tribal and frontier life, a reenactment of a stagecoach robbery, demonstrations of horseback riding and other cowboy skills, and famous sharpshooters like Annie Oakley. Cody's one-time enemy, Sioux Chief Sitting Bull, became a star attraction. After the Wild West finished touring, Cody bought a ranch east of Yellowstone and helped establish the nearby town of Cody.

JAMES CASH PENNEY
RETAILER

BORN: *September 16, 1875, Hamilton, MO*
DIED: *February 12, 1971, New York, NY*

Born in Missouri, Penney moved to Colorado at age twenty-two for his health. There he worked in a dry goods store. In 1902, Penney was sent to start a branch in Kemmerer, Wyoming. Penney saved his pennies and bought the store for himself. In five years, Penney owned three stores, which grew to five hundred by 1924. The J.C. Penney chain added links, until by 1971, there were 1,660 J.C. Penney department stores in the United States and Europe.

NELLIE DAVIS TAYLOE ROSS
GOVERNOR

BORN: *November 29, 1876, St. Joseph, MO*
DIED: *December 19, 1977, Washington, D.C.*

Ross's husband died after being elected governor of Wyoming. In 1924, Ross was elected to finish his term, becoming the first woman ever to be elected governor in the United States. In 1933, President Franklin Roosevelt named Ross director of the U.S. Mint. She was the first woman ever to hold this post. The Roosevelt dime and Jefferson nickel were introduced during Ross's term. Ross lived to be 101.

CURT GOWDY
BROADCASTER

BORN: *July 31, 1919, Green River*

Gowdy attended the University of Wyoming, then became a sportswriter and commentator on local radio. Gowdy was known as "the voice of the Boston Red Sox" for fourteen years. At NBC, Gowdy broadcast the World Series, as well as the Super Bowl and other National Football League games. He starred on ABC's *Wide World of Sports* and *American Sportsman*. In 1971, the city of Cheyenne and the Boy Scouts of America founded Curt Gowdy State Park there. In 1981, Gowdy was inducted into the National Sportscasters and Sportswriters Association Hall of Fame now located in Salisbury, North Carolina.

ALAN KOOI SIMPSON
U.S. SENATOR

BORN: *September 2, 1931, Denver, CO*

Although he was born in Denver, Simpson was raised in Cody. He played football at the University of Wyoming, then graduated from its law school in 1958. Simpson became a leading member of the Wyoming state legislature. After helping his father become governor of Wyoming, he successfully ran for the U.S. Senate in 1978. Simpson's cowboy humor and colorful personality made him an instant celebrity in Washington. Before retiring in 1997, he was a strong advocate for changing the nation's immigration laws. Simpson wrote a book published in 1997, *Right in the Old Gazoo: What I've Observed in a Lifetime of Scrapping with the American Press.*

JACKSON POLLOCK
ABSTRACT ARTIST

BORN: *January 28, 1912, Cody*
DIED: *August 12, 1956, East Hampton, NY*

Pollock moved to New York City in 1929 to study at the Art Students League. By the mid-1930s he had developed a dark, intensely personal style. Over the years, he developed new techniques that included dripping, pouring, and even flinging paint onto huge canvases on the floor. After his death in a car accident at age forty-four, Pollock became recognized as an influential figure in American art, at the forefront of the abstract expressionist movement. Examples of his work can be seen in New York's Museum of Modern Art.

Wyoming

History At-A-Glance

1500s
Arapaho, Bannock, Cheyenne, Crow, Shoshone, Sioux, and Northern Ute tribes live in the Wyoming area.

1743
France's François and Louis Joseph de La Vérendrye become first Europeans to visit Wyoming region.

1807
John Colter explores Yellowstone region.

1834
William Sublette and Robert Campbell establish Wyoming's first permanent trading post, Fort William, later called Fort Laramie.

1842
Scout Jim Bridger establishes Wyoming's second permanent settlement, Fort Bridger.

1852
Wyoming's first school opens at Fort Laramie.

1860s
Fighting breaks out between settlers and tribes along Powder River.

1863
Bozeman Trail blazes a route to Montana's mines. Wyoming's first newspaper, *The Daily Telegraph,* is established at Fort Bridger.

1867
Union Pacific Railroad enters Wyoming. Cheyenne is founded.

1868
On July 25, Congress creates the Wyoming Territory. Shoshones sign Fort Laramie Treaty: U.S. establishes Wind River Reservation.

1869
Wyoming territorial legislature gives women right to vote and hold office.

1870
On February 17, Esther Morris becomes the country's first female justice of the peace. Women first serve on a jury. Louisa Swain is first woman to vote.

1600   **1700**   **1800**

1492
Christopher Columbus comes to New World.

1607
Capt. John Smith and three ships land on Virginia coast and start first English settlement in New World — Jamestown.

1754–63
French and Indian War.

1773
Boston Tea Party.

1776
Declaration of Independence adopted July 4.

1777
Articles of Confederation adopted by Continental Congress.

1787
U.S. Constitution written.

1812–14
War of 1812.

United States

History At-A-Glance

1872
Yellowstone becomes world's first national park.

1877
Major fossil dinosaur discoveries in Wyoming spark "bone wars" between rival paleontologists Edward Cope and O. C. Marsh.

1883
Wyoming's first oil well is drilled near Lander.

1886
Laramie County Public Library is organized, first county public library in U.S. Johnson County hosts Wyoming's first county fair.

1890
On July 10, Wyoming becomes forty-fourth state.

1892
Johnson County range war breaks out (disputes between cattle barons and small ranchers).

1894
Estelle Reel is elected state superintendent of public instruction, first American woman elected to a state office.

1906
President Theodore Roosevelt makes Devils Tower first national monument.

1925
Nellie Tayloe Ross becomes first female governor in U.S. In 1933, she becomes first female director of U.S. Mint.

1951–52
Large uranium deposits are found all around Wyoming.

1977
One of the world's largest infrared telescopes is built on Jelm Mountain.

2000
Richard Cheney becomes vice president.

1800 — **1900** — **2000**

1848
Gold discovered in California draws eighty thousand prospectors in the 1849 Gold Rush.

1861–65
Civil War.

1869
Transcontinental railroad completed.

1917–18
U.S. involvement in World War I.

1929
Stock market crash ushers in Great Depression.

1941–45
U.S. involvement in World War II.

1950–53
U.S. fights in the Korean War.

1964–73
U.S. involvement in Vietnam War.

2000
George W. Bush wins the closest presidential election in history.

2001
A terrorist attack in which four hijacked airliners crash into New York City's World Trade Center, the Pentagon, and farmland in western Pennsylvania leaves thousands dead or injured.

▼ **This photo, taken in 1876, shows how Cheyenne looked to travelers along the Oregon Trail.**

Festivals and Fun for All

Check web site for exact date and directions.

1834 Ham's Fork Rendezvous, Fort Bridger

For three days in August (two weeks before Labor Day), on the site where mountain men used to gather, attendees enjoy tomahawk, knife-throwing, and shooting contests, a frying-pan toss, a parade, a contest for best 1840s costume, and more.
www.fortbridger
rendezvous.com

Buffalo Bill Birthday Ball and Annual Buffalo Bill Skijoring Races Weekend, Cody

Celebrate the birthday of the town's founder with a ball on the weekend closest to February 26 in the Cody Auditorium. The birthday bash also includes food, shooting exhibitions, and turn-of-the-century dress. Meanwhile, horses, riders, and skiers provide unique outdoor entertainment just east of Cody in nearby Stampede Park.
www.codychamber.org/
calendar/calendar.
asp?Calendar=3

Casper Mountain Sled Dog Race, Casper

Dog races raise money for Canines for Charity during two days in January on Casper Mountain's Beartrap Meadow.
www.casperwyoming.info

Fort Fetterman Powwow Days, Douglas

For one to two days during the second week of June, Douglas hosts historical reenactments, complete with cannons, campsites, and demonstrations of equipment and guns. Tour the fort — including its cemetery — and enjoy period food, like buffalo roast.
www.jackalope.org

Free Coal Mine Tours, Gillette

Monday through Friday all summer long, the largest coal producer in the nation offers free daily tours of a coal mine. Special tours available in the off-season.
www.visitgillette.net

Gift of the Waters Pageant Weekend, Thermopolis

During the first weekend in August, Thermopolis celebrates the gift of the town's amazing hot springs with local music, a Native American ceremony, two parades, the main pageant, and crafts at Hot Springs State Park.
www.thermopolis/
statepark.html.com

Horse-Drawn Carriage Rides, Cheyenne

From June through the end of August, Cheyenne offers horse-drawn carriage rides through downtown. Enjoy the ride and learn exciting local history.
www.cheyenne.org

International Pedigree Stage Stop Sled Dog Race, 13 Wyoming towns

Since 1995, the largest sled dog race in the lower forty-eight states has traveled nearly 450 miles (724 km) through thirteen Wyoming towns in ten days, starting in Jackson in late January.
www.wyomingstagestop.org

Jackson Hole Fall Arts Festival, Jackson

For ten days in September, more than thirty galleries host exhibits, auctions, and sales; a miniatures show; and concerts.
www.jacksonholechamber.com

Kids' Dig, Thermopolis

Several times each summer, children get a chance to participate in real dinosaur digs on the Warren Springs Ranch dig sites near Thermopolis. Tour the Wyoming Dinosaur Center, work in a fossil prep room, dig for dinosaur bones, and more. Visit the web site to register and learn more details.
www.wyodino.org

Riverton Rendezvous Balloon Rally, Riverton

During two weekends in July, people flock to Riverton to watch, and even help launch, huge hot-air balloons. The big picnic features a sandwich-making contest. Fireworks and a street dance add to the fun.
www.rivertonchamber.org

Rockpile Museum, Gillette

Built near a huge rock pile that became a landmark, this museum offers year-round fun, including dipping candles, making butter, and much more.
www.visitgillette.net

Winterfest, Dubois

In January, Dubois hosts a local hootenanny: dog sledding, skijoring, and chariot and bed races; a dog parade; storytelling; and a chili cook-off.
www.duboiswyoming.org

Wyoming State Fair & Rodeo, Douglas

This August event began in 1905 and features a rodeo, carnival, agricultural and industrial exhibits, and the Pioneer Museum.
www.wystatefair.com

▶ A Wyoming cowboy pulls down a steer in a bulldogging competition.

Books

Critters of Wyoming Pocket Guide. Beverly, MA: Adventure Publications, 2001.

Fox, Mary Virginia. *The Story of Women Who Shaped the West* (Cornerstones of Freedom Series). Danbury, CT: Children's Press, 1994.

Smith, Robert B., and Lee J. Siegel. *Windows Into the Earth: The Geologic Story of Yellowstone and Grand Teton National Parks*. New York: Oxford University Press, 2000.

Smith, Scott T. (photographer). *Along Wyoming's Continental Divide Trail* (The Continental Divide Trail Series). Englewood, CO: Westcliffe, 2000.

Wooldridge, Connie Nordhielm. *When Esther Morris Headed West: Women, Wyoming and the Right to Vote*. New York: Holiday House, 2001.

Web Sites

▶ Wyoming official state web site
www.state.wy.us

▶ Wyoming State Archives
http://wyoarchives.state.wy.us

▶ About Wyoming
www.wyomingtourism.org
www.wyolinks.com

Note: Page numbers in *italics* refer to maps, illustrations, or photographs.